vegetable
side dishes

vegetable
side dishes

RYLAND
PETERS
& SMALL
LONDON NEW YORK

Designer **Luana Gobbo**

Commissioning Editor **Elsa Petersen-Schepelern**

Editor **Sharon Ashman**

Production **Patricia Harrington**

Art Director **Gabriella Le Grazie**

Publishing Director **Alison Starling**

Published in the United Kingdom in 2004
by Ryland Peters & Small
Kirkman House
12–14 Whitfield Street
London W1T 2RP
www.rylandpeters.com

10 9 8 7 6 5 4 3 2 1

Text © Celia Brooks Brown, Maxine Clark, Jane
Noraika, Louise Pickford, Laura Washburn and
Lesley Waters 2004
Design and photographs © Ryland Peters & Small 2004

ISBN 1 84172 720 2

A catalogue record for this book is available from the
British Library.

Printed in China.

Notes

All spoon measurements are level.

All eggs are large, unless otherwise specified.
Uncooked or partly cooked eggs should not be served
to the very young, the very old, those with
compromised immune systems, or to pregnant women.

contents

introduction   6

beans, greens & florets   8

potatoes   26

roots & stalks   36

tomatoes, aubergines
& squash   50

index   64

credits   64

introduction

From greens to beans, squash to potatoes, vegetable side dishes add colour, texture and fresh flavours to a meal. Steamed vegetables are great, but sometimes it's appealing to jazz up your side dishes and cook something extra special. There's so much you can do to transform your vegetables – barbecue, grill, oven-bake, braise or roast them. Cover them in a creamy, warming sauce, add fresh herbs or marinate them to add flavour. However you like to cook them, there is a recipe here to suit, and lots of inspiration if you don't know where to start.

There are Italian, French and Thai-inspired recipes, full of exciting flavours, as well as old favourites. Those people who aren't keen on vegetables will undoubtedly be tempted if you serve up these delicious ideas. They are a great way of increasing your family's intake of fresh vegetables, along with all the health benefits they bring.

Although most vegetables are available nearly all year round, think about using those that are local and seasonal in order to benefit from the best flavour and freshness. This book gives you ideas for every season, from something light and fresh for summer, such as Asparagus and Lemon with Smoked Garlic Mayonnaise, to something warm and soothing for winter, like Creamy Potato Gratin.

With vegetables dishes this tasty, why let them sit on the sidelines? Let them take centre stage. In fact, many of the recipes would make great starters served on their own or main course alternatives for vegetarians. So choose a recipe and make your vegetables the stars of the show!

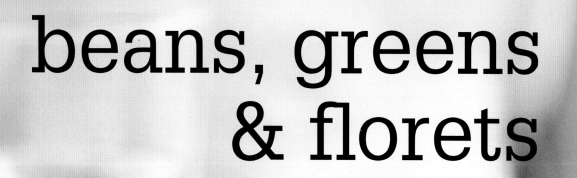

beans, greens & florets

green beans in tomato sauce

Good served hot or cold, this Italian recipe is stunning in its simplicity. It can be served as an accompaniment to a main dish or as a starter.

Put the olive and chilli oils and garlic in a large saucepan and heat until the garlic has turned very lightly golden. Stir in the tomatoes, 250 ml water and a generous pinch of salt. Bring to the boil, then add the beans. Cover with a lid and cook gently for 30–40 minutes, stirring occasionally, until the beans are very tender.

4 tablespoons olive oil

1 teaspoon chilli oil

1 garlic clove, crushed

800 g canned chopped tomatoes

600 g green beans, topped

sea salt

SERVES 4

French beans are the classic accompaniment for lamb, but they are equally delicious with fish and chicken. You can also serve them at room temperature, as part of a salad buffet. Instead of the cooked beans, try long, thin slices of steamed courgettes, sautéed with the garlic.

french beans with garlic

625 g small green beans, topped

2 tablespoons extra virgin olive oil

1 tablespoon unsalted butter

2 garlic cloves, crushed

a handful of flat leaf parsley, chopped

1 teaspoon freshly squeezed lemon juice (optional)

coarse sea salt and freshly ground black pepper

SERVES 4

Bring a large saucepan of water to the boil. Add the beans, return to the boil and cook for 3–4 minutes. Drain and refresh under cold running water. Set aside.

Heat the oil and butter in a frying pan. Add the garlic, beans and salt and cook over high heat for 1 minute, stirring. Remove from the heat and stir in the parsley and lemon juice, if using. Sprinkle with pepper and serve.

Variation Flageolet beans are the other traditional partner for lamb. Generally, dried beans taste better if cooked from scratch, but this does require advance planning. Happily, flageolets are the exception, especially if you can find imported French flageolets in jars, not cans. For mixed beans to serve with lamb (for four), halve the quantity of green beans and add a 400 g jar of drained flageolet beans to the cooked green beans when frying with the garlic. Instead of lemon juice, stir in 3–4 tablespoons crème fraîche just before serving.

Beans were traditionally cooked this way in Tuscany when Chianti flasks were plentiful and blown from one piece of glass. The flask was embedded in the glowing ashes of the hearth to cook for as long as possible. You can use a casserole dish in the oven – it's just not as romantic.

beans simmered in a chianti flask

400 g small dried cannellini beans

2 garlic cloves, unpeeled

6–8 fresh sage leaves

10 tablespoons extra virgin olive oil, plus extra for sprinkling

sea salt and freshly ground black pepper

an ovenproof casserole dish or beanpot, or a hand-blown Chianti flask and a roasting tin

a circle of greaseproof paper (see method), plus extra greaseproof paper or muslin

SERVES 4

Put the beans in an ovenproof casserole, beanpot or hand-blown Chianti flask – don't use a modern moulded flask with a seam, because it may crack. Add the whole unpeeled garlic cloves, sage, olive oil, salt and pepper. Pour in enough warm water to fill the flask three-quarters full – or, if using a casserole dish or beanpot, pour in 3 times the volume of the other ingredients.

Plug the neck of the flask with scrunched up greaseproof paper or with rolled and folded muslin – this lets the contents 'breathe' and stops the flask exploding. If using a casserole or beanpot, make sure it has a tight-fitting lid.

Put the flask on its side in a roasting tin half-filled with hot water and cook in a preheated oven at 160°C (325°F) Gas 3 for 3 hours, turning every now and then. If using a casserole dish or beanpot, cover with a lid and put it in the oven at the same temperature and cook for 2 hours, then put a circle of greaseproof paper directly on top of the beans to keep in the moisture. Cover and return to the oven for another hour. The beans must be very tender and absorb most of the water and oil.

When cooked, transfer the beans to a heated serving dish and dress liberally with olive oil. Taste and season with salt and pepper. This dish is best served hot, with Italian sausages or roast pork, or as a simple first course with bread.

spinach flan

This recipe is inspired by a side dish from the Jura region of France, which was made from a mixture of vegetables all thinly sliced and baked in a fabulous savoury custard. Here, just spinach is used, but you could add a selection of vegetables of your choice, if you were feeling creative. It makes a particularly delicious accompaniment to roast pork.

Wash the spinach, then spin-dry in a salad spinner. Working in batches, heat 1 tablespoon of the oil in a non-stick frying pan and add a mound of spinach. Cook the spinach over high heat, stirring until all the leaves have just wilted. Transfer to a plastic colander and let drain. Continue cooking until all the spinach has been wilted.

Chop the spinach coarsely. Put the crème fraîche, eggs, salt and nutmeg in a bowl and whisk well. Stir in the spinach.

Spread the butter over the bottom of the baking dish. Transfer the spinach mixture to the dish and bake in a preheated oven at 180°C (350°F) Gas 4 until just set, 25–30 minutes. Serve hot.

500 g fresh spinach

3–5 tablespoons extra virgin olive oil

200 ml crème fraîche

2 eggs

1 teaspoon coarse sea salt

a pinch of freshly grated nutmeg

1 tablespoon unsalted butter

a baking dish, about 30 cm long or 22 cm diameter

SERVES 4

broccoli trees
with pan-fried pine nuts

500 g broccoli

25 g butter

50 g pine nuts

**sea salt and freshly
ground black pepper**

SERVES 4

Cut the broccoli into medium florets, leaving a long
stalk. Put in a large, microwave-safe bowl, add
50 ml water, cover with microwave-safe clingfilm
or a lid and microwave on HIGH for 3 minutes.
Alternatively, steam the broccoli for 4–5 minutes.

Meanwhile, put the butter, pine nuts and salt and
pepper to taste in a small saucepan over medium
heat. Cook for 2–3 minutes until the nuts are golden
and the butter is foaming.

Drain the broccoli through a colander or sieve, return
to the bowl and toss with the pine nuts and butter.
Serve immediately or let cool and serve as a salad.

This is about as speedy as good
cooking gets! Broccoli is ideal for the
microwave, as the stalks and florets
cook evenly and don't go soggy.

A regular accompaniment on the *plat du jour* circuit in French bistros, this recipe goes especially well with pork. The secret of delicious cauliflower is to blanch it first; if you add a bay leaf to the water, the unpleasant cabbage aroma disappears.

cauliflower gratin

1 fresh bay leaf

1 large cauliflower, separated into large florets

500 ml double cream

2 teaspoons Dijon mustard

1 teaspoon coarse sea salt, plus extra for adding to the boiling water

1 egg

160 g finely grated Comté cheese*

a baking dish, about 25 cm diameter, greased with butter

SERVES 4–6

Bring a large saucepan of water to the boil, add the bay leaf, salt generously, then add the cauliflower. Cook until still slightly firm, about 10 minutes. Drain and set aside.

Put the cream in a saucepan and bring to the boil. Boil for 10 minutes, then stir in the mustard and the 1 teaspoon salt.

Divide the cauliflower into smaller florets, then stir into the cream sauce with the egg. Transfer to the prepared baking dish and sprinkle the cheese over the top in an even layer. Bake in a preheated oven at 200°C (400°F) Gas 6 until golden, about 40–45 minutes. Serve hot.

*Note Use Emmental or Cantal cheese if Comté is unavailable.

sardinian cauliflower with olives

This is a spectacular way to serve a whole creamy head of cauliflower. Let your guests serve themselves, pulling out the florets. There's no fuss needed for this gloriously simple dish.

1 large whole cauliflower, green leaves removed and reserved

2 onions, finely chopped

300 g small green pitted olives

6 tablespoons olive oil, plus extra to serve

sea salt

a small bunch of flat leaf parsley, finely chopped, to serve

SERVES 4

Line a large, heavy-based saucepan with the reserved outer leaves from the cauliflower. Put the cauliflower on top. Sprinkle with the onion, olives and some salt, then pour over the 6 tablespoons olive oil.

Cover with a lid, set over the lowest heat and cook gently for about 40 minutes or until tender – there should be no resistance when a fork is inserted into the middle of the cauliflower.

Carefully lift the cauliflower out of the saucepan and onto a large plate – be very careful not to break it. Pile the onion and olives on top, then sprinkle with the parsley and more olive oil and serve.

braised red cabbage with chestnuts and apples

This red cabbage recipe includes apples, chestnuts, Alsatian Riesling as well as bacon. Serve it with grilled sausages, pork chops or roasts, and a glass or two of the same wine used in the cooking. It is also fantastic with Christmas goose.

1 red cabbage

3 tablespoons unsalted butter

1 onion, halved and thinly sliced

75 g bacon lardons

3 cooking apples, peeled, cored and chopped

200 g vacuum-packed whole peeled chestnuts

2 teaspoons coarse sea salt

250 ml dry white wine, preferably Riesling

1 tablespoon sugar

SERVES 4–6

Cut the cabbage in quarters, then core and slice thinly.

Melt 2 tablespoons of the butter in a sauté pan. Add the onion and lardons and cook until soft, about 3 minutes.

Add the remaining butter, the cabbage, apples and chestnuts and stir well. Season with salt, then add the wine, sugar and 250 ml water.

Bring to the boil, boil for 1 minute, then cover and simmer gently until the cabbage is tender, about 45 minutes. Serve hot.

This hybrid Thai coleslaw is based on the classic *som tum*, usually made from grated green papaya (when unripe, the fruit is firm, crunchy and perfect for grating). Green papaya is not the easiest ingredient to find, so red cabbage is used here instead.

thai coleslaw

To make the dressing, reserve a few coriander leaves, then put the rest in a blender or food processor. Add the chillies, garlic, soy sauce, lime juice and sugar and blend until smooth. Set aside.

Blanch the beans in boiling water for 2 minutes, then refresh in cold water. Mix the cabbage, beans, tomatoes and spring onions in a bowl. Pour the dressing over the top, toss well to coat and let marinate for about 30 minutes.

Spoon into bowls lined with the lettuce leaves, if using, sprinkle with the ground peanuts and the reserved coriander leaves, then serve.

100 g green beans, topped

200 g finely shredded red or white cabbage

3 plum tomatoes, halved lengthways, deseeded and sliced

4 spring onions, sliced

50 g roasted peanuts, coarsely ground

4 cup-shaped lettuce leaves, to serve (optional)

DRESSING

a handful of fresh coriander

2 red chillies, deseeded

2 garlic cloves, chopped

2 tablespoons light soy sauce

2 tablespoons freshly squeezed lime juice

2 tablespoons palm sugar or soft brown sugar

SERVES 4

potatoes

calabrian-style potatoes and peppers

This is a fine example of the 'less is more' approach to cooking – simple, good-quality ingredients cooked to perfection.

150 ml olive oil

1 red pepper, halved, deseeded and thickly sliced

1 yellow pepper, halved, deseeded and thickly sliced

550 g potatoes, thinly sliced

sea salt and freshly ground black pepper

a small bunch of flat leaf parsley, finely chopped, to serve (optional)

SERVES 4

Heat the oil in a large, lidded frying pan. Add the red and yellow peppers and cook for 10 minutes, stirring occasionally, until starting to turn golden brown. Add the potatoes, salt and pepper to the pan, cover with a lid and cook for 5 minutes.

Remove the lid and continue cooking for 15 minutes, turning every few minutes as the potatoes begin to brown, taking care not to break them. If the potatoes start to stick, this will just add to the flavour of the dish, but don't let them burn.

When the potatoes are tender, transfer to a serving dish and top with the parsley, if using. Let cool for 5 minutes before serving.

new potato salad
with gazpacho dressing

500 g new potatoes, scrubbed
but not peeled

GAZPACHO DRESSING

2 large, ripe tomatoes, halved,
deseeded and diced

50 g preserved roasted red
peppers (in a jar), diced

½ small red onion, chopped

1 garlic clove, chopped

3 tablespoons extra virgin
olive oil

2 teaspoons red wine vinegar

a pinch of sugar

a bunch of flat leaf parsley,
coarsely chopped

sea salt and freshly ground
black pepper

SERVES 4

Gazpacho is the famous Spanish chilled soup, made with tomatoes, peppers, onions and garlic. Use the same ingredients to make a fresh dressing for this simple salad of new potatoes. Add the dressing to the potatoes while they are hot, even if you aren't eating them straight away, as this will help the flavours to infuse.

Bring a large saucepan of lightly salted water to the boil, add the potatoes and return to the boil. Reduce the heat and simmer for about 12 minutes or until the potatoes are just tender when pierced with a knife.

Meanwhile, put all the dressing ingredients in a large bowl and mix well. Add plenty of salt and pepper.

Drain the potatoes thoroughly. Add them to the dressing and toss well. Serve hot or let cool to room temperature.

Cream and potatoes, mingling in the heat of the oven, are almost all you'll find in this well-loved dish. If it had cheese, it wouldn't be truly authentic. Serve as a partner for roast meat or poultry, with a mixed green salad, or simply on its own.

creamy potato gratin

2 kg waxy salad-style potatoes, cut in half if large

2 litres whole milk

1 fresh bay leaf

30 g unsalted butter

550 ml whipping cream

a pinch of freshly grated nutmeg

coarse sea salt

a baking dish, 30 cm long

SERVES 4–6

Put the potatoes in a large saucepan with the milk and bay leaf. Bring to the boil, then lower the heat, add a pinch of salt and simmer gently until part-cooked, 5–10 minutes.

Drain the potatoes. When cool enough to handle (but still hot), slice into rounds about 3 mm thick.

Spread the butter in the bottom of the baking dish. Arrange half the potato slices in the dish and sprinkle with salt. Put the remaining potato on top and sprinkle with more salt. Pour in the cream and sprinkle with the grated nutmeg.

Bake in a preheated oven at 180°C (350°F) Gas 4 until golden and the cream is almost absorbed, but not completely, about 45 minutes. Serve hot.

potato and mushroom gratin

Baking sliced potatoes and mushrooms in layers allows the potatoes to absorb the juices and earthy flavour of the mushrooms. Use the darkest mushrooms you can find – they will have the best taste. If you prefer, you can mix fresh mushrooms with reconstituted dried ones for a more intense flavour.

Peel the potatoes and slice thickly, putting them in a bowl of cold water as you go. Trim the mushrooms and slice thickly. Put half the potatoes in a layer in the bottom of the gratin dish, sprinkle with olive oil and cover with half the mushrooms.

Put the breadcrumbs, Parmesan, parsley, salt and pepper in a bowl and mix well. Spread half this mixture over the mushrooms, then sprinkle with more olive oil. Cover with a layer of the remaining potatoes, then a layer of the remaining mushrooms. Finally, sprinkle with the remaining breadcrumb mixture and more oil.

Cover with foil and bake in a preheated oven at 180°C (350°F) Gas 4 for 30 minutes. Uncover the dish and cook for a further 30 minutes until the potatoes are tender and the breadcrumb topping is golden brown.

Note If you blanch the potato slices first for 5 minutes in boiling salted water, they will take only 30 minutes to cook in the oven.

1 kg potatoes

750 g flavoursome mushrooms, such as dark flat cap, chestnut or portobello (or use fresh wild mushrooms)

extra virgin olive oil, for sprinkling

175 g stale (not dry) white breadcrumbs

4 tablespoons freshly grated Parmesan cheese

4 tablespoons chopped fresh flat leaf parsley

sea salt and freshly ground black pepper

a deep gratin or other ovenproof dish, well buttered

SERVES 4

roasted sweet potatoes
with shallots, garlic and chillies

These crisp, golden and bravely flavoured sweet potatoes make a delicious alternative to regular roast potatoes. This recipe is for garlic and chilli lovers everywhere.

12 shallots, unpeeled

8 garlic cloves, unpeeled

1 kg orange-fleshed sweet potatoes, cut into even chunks

1 teaspoon coriander seeds, crushed

2 red chillies

6 tablespoons olive oil

sea salt and freshly ground black pepper

SERVES 4

Put the shallots and garlic in a bowl, cover with boiling water, let soak for 30 minutes, then drain and peel. The skins should slip off easily.

Transfer to a roasting tin and add the sweet potatoes, coriander seeds and whole chillies. Add the olive oil, salt and pepper and toss well to coat.

Roast in a preheated oven at 200°C (400°F) Gas 6 for 30 minutes until the potatoes are golden and tender. Shake the tin from time to time during cooking and brush the vegetables with the pan juices. Serve hot.

roots & stalks

asparagus and lemon with smoked garlic mayonnaise

The best way to enjoy asparagus is to roast or char-grill it. If you are using a charcoal barbecue, start cooking when the coals turn white, since this is when they are at their hottest. If using a stove-top grill pan, start cooking when the pan is smoking hot to maximize the asparagus flavour. To prepare asparagus, just snap off and discard the woody ends.

Heat a barbecue or stove-top grill pan until very hot.

Put the asparagus in a bowl, add the olive oil and toss to coat. Set on the hot barbecue or stove-top grill pan and cook for about 10 minutes, turning frequently, or until starting to become golden brown. Remove to a plate and sprinkle with salt and pepper. Squeeze the lemon juice over the top before serving.

Stir the smoked garlic into the mayonnaise and serve as an accompaniment.

24 asparagus spears

2–3 tablespoons olive oil

sea salt and freshly ground black pepper

freshly squeezed juice of ½ lemon, to serve

SMOKED GARLIC MAYONNAISE

3–4 smoked garlic cloves, crushed

4 tablespoons mayonnaise

SERVES 4

For this dish you need beetroots and baby onions of roughly the same size, so they will cook evenly on the barbecue. They make an excellent accompaniment to grilled meats or salads.

beetroot and baby onion brochettes

32 large fresh bay leaves

20 small beetroot

20 baby onions, unpeeled

3 tablespoons extra virgin olive oil

1 tablespoon balsamic vinegar

sea salt and freshly ground black pepper

8 metal skewers

SERVES 4

Put the bay leaves in a bowl, cover with cold water and let soak for 1 hour before cooking.

Cut the stalks off the beetroot and wash well under cold running water. Bring a large saucepan of lightly salted water to the boil, add the beetroot and baby onions and blanch for 5 minutes. Drain and refresh under cold running water. Pat dry with kitchen paper, then peel the onions.

Preheat a barbecue. Thread the beetroot, onions and damp bay leaves onto the skewers, sprinkle with the olive oil and vinegar and season well with salt and pepper. Cook over medium-hot coals for 20–25 minutes, turning occasionally, until charred and tender, then serve immediately.

In this recipe, thyme transforms ordinary boiled carrots into something subtly sumptuous. The crème fraîche helps too. You can substitute steamed baby leeks for the carrots, but stir in a tablespoon of butter when adding the crème fraîche.

carrots with crème fraîche and herbs

800 g mini carrots, trimmed, or medium carrots

50 g unsalted butter

a sprig of thyme

2 tablespoons crème fraîche

several sprigs of chervil

a small bunch of chives

fine sea salt

SERVES 4

If using larger carrots, cut them diagonally into 5 cm slices. Put in a large saucepan (the carrots should fit in almost a single layer for even cooking). Add the butter and set over low heat. Cook to melt and coat, about 3 minutes. Half-fill the saucepan with water, then add a pinch of salt and the thyme. Cover and cook until the water is almost completely evaporated, 10–20 minutes.

Stir in the crème fraîche and add salt to taste. Using kitchen scissors, snip the chervil and chives over the top, mix well and serve.

Variation In spring, when turnips are sweet, they make a great addition to this dish. Peel and quarter large turnips, or just peel baby ones and leave them whole – the main thing is to ensure that all the vegetable pieces (carrots and turnips) are about the same size so that they cook evenly. Halve the carrot quantity and complete with turnips, or double the recipe. Sprinkle with a large handful of just-cooked peas before serving for extra crunch and colour.

Tarator, the nut sauce served with these leeks, is found in Middle Eastern cooking, though cooks there would use ground almonds or walnuts. If the sauce is made in advance, whisk well before you use it.

750 g baby leeks, trimmed

2–3 tablespoons extra virgin olive oil

sea salt

a few lemon wedges, to serve

TARATOR SAUCE

50 g macadamia nuts, toasted

25 g fresh breadcrumbs

2 garlic cloves, crushed

100 ml extra virgin olive oil

1 tablespoon freshly squeezed lemon juice

2 tablespoons boiling water

sea salt and freshly ground black pepper

SERVES 4

charred leeks with tarator sauce

To make the sauce, put the nuts in a food processor and blend coarsely, then add the breadcrumbs, garlic, salt and pepper and process again to form a smooth paste. Transfer to a bowl and very gradually whisk in the olive oil, lemon juice and the 2 tablespoons boiling water to form a sauce. Season to taste with salt and pepper.

Preheat a barbecue or stove-top grill pan. Brush the leeks with a little olive oil, season with salt and cook over medium heat for 6–10 minutes, turning occasionally, until charred and tender. Transfer to a serving plate, sprinkle with olive oil, then pour the sauce over the top and serve with the lemon wedges.

Fresh peas with lettuce form one of the classics of French cuisine. Teamed with asparagus in a light buttery sauce, they're ideal for serving with roast poultry or grilled fish. Bacon makes a nice addition so you can also stir in about 75 g fried bacon lardons, just before serving. If chervil is unavailable, use finely chopped flat leaf parsley.

asparagus, peas and baby lettuce

75 g unsalted butter

3–4 small shallots, sliced into rounds

3 Little Gem lettuces, quartered

100 g asparagus tips, halved lengthways

400 g shelled fresh peas

coarse sea salt

sprigs of chervil or snipped chives, to serve

SERVES 4

Melt half the butter in a saucepan with a lid. Add the shallots and lettuce and cook, covered, stirring often, until tender, 8–10 minutes.

Season with salt, add the remaining butter and the asparagus and cook for 5 minutes.

Add the peas, cover and cook for 3 minutes more. Taste for seasoning, sprinkle with the herbs and serve.

Variation For a more substantial vegetable side dish or even a light meal, add 300 g sliced baby carrots and a splash of water when cooking the lettuce. Before serving, gently stir in more butter or 1 tablespoon crème fraîche and add 500 g boiled small new potatoes, sliced into wedges. Be sure to cook the potatoes in salted water or they will be bland.

Poor old celery; it is more often an ingredient than the star of a dish. However, in this traditional Provençal recipe, it takes centre stage. Beef is the ideal complement to the trinity of celery, tomatoes and anchovies, so serve this with roast beef or grilled steaks.

braised celery

2 whole heads of celery

2 tablespoons extra virgin olive oil

75 g bacon lardons

1 onion, quartered and sliced

1 carrot, quartered lengthways and sliced

2 garlic cloves, sliced

200 g canned chopped tomatoes

250 ml dry white wine

1 fresh bay leaf

50 g canned anchovy fillets, about 8, chopped

a handful of flat leaf parsley, chopped

coarse sea salt and freshly ground black pepper

SERVES 4–6

Remove any tough outer stalks from the celery and trim the tips so they will just fit into a large sauté pan with a lid.

Bring a large saucepan of water to the boil. Add a pinch of salt, then the celery and simmer gently for 10 minutes to blanch. Remove, drain and pat dry with kitchen paper.

Heat the oil in the sauté pan. Add the bacon lardons, onion and carrot and cook gently until lightly browned. Add the celery and a little salt and pepper and cook just to brown, then remove.

Add the garlic, cook for 1 minute, then add the tomatoes, wine and bay leaf. Bring to the boil and cook for 1 minute. Add the celery, cover and simmer gently for 30 minutes, turning the celery once during cooking.

Transfer the celery to a serving dish. Raise the heat and cook the sauce to reduce it slightly, about 10 minutes. Pour it over the celery, sprinkle with the anchovies and parsley and serve.

grilled corn-on-the-cob

In this version of the famous recipe, corn-on-the-cob steams inside the husks first, then has a short blast over hot coals to brown and flavour the kernels. Delicious served with this zesty herb butter.

4 corn cobs, unhusked

125 g butter

1 garlic clove, crushed

2 teaspoons chopped fresh thyme

grated zest of 1 unwaxed lemon

sea salt and freshly ground black pepper

SERVES 4

Carefully peel back the husks from the corn, but leave them attached at the stalk. Remove and discard the cornsilk. Fold the husks back in position and tie in place with string. Put the corn in a large bowl of cold water, let soak for 30 minutes, then drain and pat dry with kitchen paper.

Preheat a barbecue, then cook the corn over medium-hot coals for 15 minutes, turning regularly until the outer husks are evenly charred. Remove from the heat, let cool slightly, then remove the husks. Return to the grill rack and cook for a further 8–10 minutes, turning frequently until the kernels are lightly charred.

Meanwhile, put the butter, garlic, thyme, lemon zest, salt and pepper in a small saucepan and heat gently until the butter has melted. Sprinkle the butter mixture over the cooked corn and serve.

tomatoes, aubergines & squash

courgettes and tomatoes baked with fontina

Courgettes are much more flavourful when cooked this way – bathed in garlic and olive oil, then stuffed with sweet, ripe cherry tomatoes and enveloped in melting fontina cheese. Delightfully fresh and summery.

Halve the courgettes lengthways and trim a little off the uncut sides so that they will sit still like boats. Using a teaspoon, scoop out the soft-seeded centres. Arrange the boats in a row in the prepared dish.

Put the garlic, olive oil, salt and pepper in a bowl, stir well, then brush over the cut surfaces of the courgettes. Arrange the halved tomatoes in the grooves. Season well with salt and pepper, then sprinkle with olive oil and breadcrumbs. Bake in a preheated oven at 160°C (325°F) Gas 3 for 30 minutes.

Remove from the oven and arrange the cheese over the courgettes and tomatoes. Return the dish to the oven for another 10 minutes to melt the cheese. Serve immediately while the cheese is still bubbling.

6 medium courgettes (as straight as possible)

2 garlic cloves, chopped

2 tablespoons olive oil, plus extra for sprinkling

about 30 cherry tomatoes, halved

3–4 tablespoons dried breadcrumbs

250 g fontina cheese, sliced

sea salt and freshly ground black pepper

a shallow ovenproof dish, greased

SERVES 6

aubergine, tomato and parmesan gratin

A pretty gratin bursting with flavour. Tomato halves are baked with briefly fried, thinly sliced aubergines and freshly grated Parmesan.

Cut the aubergine lengthways into 5 mm slices. Sprinkle with salt and let drain in a colander for 30 minutes. Rinse well and pat dry with kitchen paper. Cut the tomatoes in half through the middle.

Heat the oil in a frying pan and fry the aubergines in batches until deep golden brown. Drain on kitchen paper. Arrange a layer of aubergines in the prepared dish, then top with the tomato halves, cut side up. Sprinkle with the chopped basil, salt, pepper and half the Parmesan. Add another layer of aubergines, then sprinkle with the remaining Parmesan.

Bake in a preheated oven at 200°C (400°F) Gas 6 for 20–25 minutes or until browned and bubbling on top. Let cool slightly and serve warm, or let cool completely and serve as a salad.

1 large aubergine

500 g very ripe, red tomatoes

about 150 ml olive oil

4 tablespoons freshly chopped basil

125 g freshly grated Parmesan cheese

sea salt and freshly ground black pepper

a shallow ovenproof dish, well buttered

SERVES 4

beef tomatoes
with garlic and herb butter

To be enjoyed at their best, beef tomatoes should be eaten hot and preferably in season. They make a great focal point for any meal and their lack of pretension is hugely appealing.

Remove the stalk from each tomato and carefully cut out a small cavity for the filling.

Put the garlic, butter, chilli oil, parsley and pepper in a bowl and mix well. Fill the tomato cavities with the garlic mixture, pressing down gently as you go. Put on the baking tray, sprinkle with olive oil, and roast in a preheated oven at 150°C (300°F) Gas 2 for 1 hour 20 minutes.

Remove from the oven and serve hot with some of the cooking juices poured over the top.

4 beef tomatoes

3 garlic cloves, crushed

70 g unsalted butter, softened

1 teaspoon chilli oil

a large handful of flat leaf parsley, finely chopped

freshly ground black pepper

olive oil, for sprinkling

a baking tray

SERVES 4

ratatouille

1 kg aubergines, cut into
3–4 cm pieces

extra virgin olive oil (see method)

2 medium onions,
coarsely chopped

2 red peppers, halved, deseeded
and cut into 3–4 cm pieces

2 yellow peppers, halved,
deseeded and cut into
3–4 cm pieces

1 green pepper, halved,
deseeded and cut into
3–4 cm pieces

6 smallish courgettes,
about 750 g, halved lengthways
and sliced

4 garlic cloves, crushed

6 medium tomatoes, halved,
deseeded and chopped

a small bunch of basil,
coarsely chopped

coarse sea salt

TO SERVE

a few basil leaves, thinly sliced

1 garlic clove, crushed

SERVES 4–6

This method for making ratatouille involves adding each vegetable separately, in the order which best suits their cooking requirements, rather than all at the same time. It does make a difference. It is also important to season each vegetable 'layer' individually.

Put the aubergine pieces in a microwave-proof bowl with 3 tablespoons water and microwave on HIGH for 6 minutes. Drain and set aside.

Heat 3 tablespoons of oil in a large casserole with a lid. Add the onions and cook until soft, 3–5 minutes. Salt lightly.

Add all the peppers and cook for 5–8 minutes more, stirring often. Turn up the heat to keep the sizzling sound going, but take care not to let it burn. Salt lightly.

Add 1 more tablespoon of oil and the courgettes. Mix well and cook for about 5 minutes more, stirring occasionally. Salt lightly.

Add 2 more tablespoons of oil and the drained aubergines. Cook, stirring often, for 5 minutes more. Salt lightly.

Add the garlic and cook for 1 minute. Add 1 more tablespoon of oil if necessary, and the tomatoes and basil and stir well. Salt lightly. Cook for 5 minutes, then cover, lower the heat and simmer gently for 30 minutes, checking occasionally.

Remove the casserole from the heat. This is best served at room temperature, but it still tastes good hot. The longer you let it stand, the richer it tastes. Stir in extra basil and garlic just before serving.

Turn ordinary vegetables into something fabulous with this gorgeous Thai-flavoured sauce. Use it as a marinade here, but also try it as a ketchup – on burgers or on hot dogs. The sauce will keep for up to a week if kept in an airtight container in the refrigerator.

thai-glazed vegetable skewers

To make the sauce, put the creamed coconut in a bowl, add 3 tablespoons boiling water and dissolve to make a thick paste. Transfer to a blender or food processor, add the remaining sauce ingredients and blend until smooth.

Peel the mango with a sharp knife and stand it upright on a board, narrow end pointing up. Slice off thick cheeks parallel to the stone and cut off strips around the stone. Cut the flesh into equal chunks.

Thread the skewers with the fruit and vegetable chunks, each starting and ending with a lime leaf, if using. Brush the sauce generously over the loaded skewers, then cover and let marinate in the refrigerator for at least 30 minutes. Reserve the remaining sauce.

Put the skewers on a hot barbecue or stove-top grill pan, or under a preheated grill, and cook, turning occasionally and basting with the remaining sauce, until tender and lightly charred.

1 large, firm, ripe mango

1 yellow pepper, deseeded and cut into 10 pieces

2 small red onions, cut into 10 wedges

2 small courgettes, cut into 10 pieces

1–2 limes, cut into 10 slices

10 button mushrooms

1 red pepper, deseeded and cut into 10 pieces

5 chillies, halved (optional)

20 kaffir lime leaves (optional)

THAI BARBECUE SAUCE

50 g block creamed coconut, chopped

75 ml dark soy sauce

2 tablespoons soft brown sugar

2 tablespoons rice wine vinegar or freshly squeezed lime juice

3 tablespoons tomato purée

3 kaffir lime leaves, chopped

1 lemongrass stalk, thinly sliced

1–2 bird's eye chillies, sliced

1 fat garlic clove, sliced

2 tablespoons sunflower oil

10 metal or long bamboo skewers (if bamboo, soak in water for 30 minutes)

MAKES 10

When pumpkin is in season, it often appears on menus as a gratin in the south of France. The conventional recipe is simply a purée with béchamel and a topping of crisp, browned breadcrumbs. This version has rice, which gives it a more interesting texture and makes it substantial enough to be a meal on its own, served with a green salad.

pumpkin and rice gratin

Peel and deseed the pumpkin and cut into small cubes. Put in a large saucepan with 2 tablespoons of the oil, a pinch of salt and 250 ml water. Cook over low heat, stirring often and adding more water as necessary, until soft, about 20–30 minutes.

Meanwhile, put the rice and the remaining 1 tablespoon oil in another saucepan and cook over medium heat, stirring to coat the grains. Add 250 ml water, a pinch of salt and the thyme sprig and bring to the boil. Cover and simmer until almost tender, about 10 minutes, then drain and discard the thyme.

Mix the breadcrumbs with the parsley and a pinch of salt.

Squash the cooked pumpkin into a coarse purée with a wooden spoon and stir in the rice and crème fraîche. Taste; the topping and cheese will add flavour, but the pumpkin should be seasoned with salt and pepper as well.

Spoon the pumpkin mixture into the prepared baking dish and spread evenly. Sprinkle the cheese in a thin layer over the top, then follow with a layer of the breadcrumbs. Bake in a preheated oven at 200°C (400°F) Gas 6 until browned, about 20–30 minutes. Serve hot.

1.5 kg pumpkin

3 tablespoons extra virgin olive oil

100 g long grain rice

a sprig of thyme

3 tablespoons fresh breadcrumbs

a small handful of flat leaf parsley, finely chopped

3 tablespoons crème fraîche

75 g finely grated Gruyère cheese

coarse sea salt and freshly ground black pepper

a large baking dish, greased with unsalted butter

SERVES 8

courgettes and patty pans infused with mint and balsamic vinegar

If you think that grilled food is predictable, this dish will change your opinion and prove to be a refreshing change. It looks and tastes sunny and fresh – you can prepare it in advance, then leave the vegetables to soak up the oil, mint and balsamic vinegar. Delicious.

Put the patty pans on a preheated barbecue or stove-top grill pan. Cook on each side for about 5 minutes or until tender, turning over when starting to char.

When cooked, transfer to a serving dish. Pour over the oil and vinegar and sprinkle with pine nuts, mint, salt and pepper.

Cook the sliced courgettes on the barbecue or in the pan for just 1–2 minutes each side. Add to the patty pan mixture and turn to coat. Cover and let marinate for about 2 hours in the refrigerator, then serve.

Note Patty pans are members of the squash family and are yellow or green. They look a little alien, rather like mini flying saucers, but taste wonderful. They are available from large supermarkets all summer.

400 g yellow and green patty pans, cut in half

6 tablespoons olive oil

2 tablespoons balsamic vinegar

40 g pine nuts, lightly toasted in a dry frying pan

a handful of fresh mint leaves, coarsely chopped

3 courgettes (about 500 g), cut lengthways into 5 mm slices

sea salt and freshly ground black pepper

SERVES 4

index

Apples, braised red cabbage with chestnuts and, 23
asparagus: asparagus and lemon with smoked garlic mayonnaise, 37
asparagus, peas and baby lettuce, 45
aubergines: aubergine, tomato and Parmesan gratin, 52
ratatouille, 56

Barbecue sauce, Thai, 59
beetroot and baby onion brochettes, 38
broccoli trees with pan-fried pine nuts, 16

Cabbage: braised red cabbage with chestnuts and apples, 23
Thai coleslaw, 24
Calabrian-style potatoes and peppers, 27
cannellini beans: beans simmered in a Chianti flask, 12
carrots with crème fraîche and herbs, 41
cauliflower: cauliflower gratin, 19
Sardinian cauliflower with olives, 20
celery, braised, 47
cheese: aubergine, tomato and Parmesan gratin, 52
cauliflower gratin, 19
courgettes and tomatoes baked with fontina, 51
chestnuts, braised red cabbage with apples and, 23
chillies, roasted sweet potatoes with shallots, garlic and, 35
coleslaw, Thai, 24
corn-on-the-cob, grilled, 48
courgettes: courgettes and patty pans infused with mint and balsamic vinegar, 63
courgettes and tomatoes baked with fontina, 51

Flageolet beans with garlic, 11
flan, spinach, 15

French beans with garlic, 11

Garlic: asparagus and lemon with smoked garlic mayonnaise, 37
beef tomatoes with garlic and herb butter, 55
roasted sweet potatoes with shallots, chillies and, 35
gratins: aubergine, tomato and Parmesan, 52
cauliflower, 19
creamy potato, 31
potato and mushroom, 32
pumpkin and rice, 60
green beans: French beans with garlic, 11
green beans in tomato sauce, 9

Leeks: charred leeks with tarator sauce, 42
lettuce: asparagus, peas and baby lettuce, 45

Mayonnaise, smoked garlic, 37
mushrooms: potato and mushroom gratin, 32

Olives, Sardinian cauliflower with, 20
onions: beetroot and baby onion brochettes, 38

Patty pans: courgettes and patty pans infused with mint and balsamic vinegar, 63
peas, asparagus and baby lettuce, 45
peppers: Calabrian-style potatoes and, 27
ratatouille, 56
pine nuts: broccoli trees with pan-fried pine nuts, 16
potatoes: Calabrian-style peppers and, 27
creamy potato gratin, 31
new potato salad with gazpacho dressing, 28
potato and mushroom gratin, 32
pumpkin and rice gratin, 60

Ratatouille, 56
red cabbage: braised red cabbage with chestnuts and apples, 23
Thai coleslaw, 24
rice and pumpkin gratin, 60

Salad, new potato, 28
Sardinian cauliflower with olives, 20
shallots, roasted sweet potatoes with garlic, chillies and, 35
spinach flan, 15
sweet potatoes with shallots, garlic and chillies, 35

Thai coleslaw, 24
Thai-glazed vegetable skewers, 59
tomatoes: aubergine, tomato and Parmesan gratin, 52
beef tomatoes with garlic and herb butter, 55
braised celery, 47
courgettes and tomatoes baked with fontina, 51
green beans in tomato sauce, 9
new potato salad with gazpacho dressing, 28

credits

RECIPES
Celia Brooks Brown
Thai coleslaw
Thai-glazed vegetable skewers
Roasted sweet potatoes with shallots, garlic and chillies
Maxine Clark
Courgettes and tomatoes baked with fontina
Aubergine, tomato and Parmesan gratin
Potato and mushroom gratin
Beans simmered in a Chianti flask
Jane Noraika
Asparagus and lemon with smoked garlic mayonnaise

Calabrian-style potatoes and peppers
Beef tomatoes with garlic and herb butter
Green beans in tomato sauce
Sardinian cauliflower with olives
Courgettes and patty pans infused with mint and balsamic vinegar
Louise Pickford
Grilled corn-on-the-cob
Beetroot and baby onion brochettes
Charred leeks with tarator sauce
Laura Washburn
Braised celery
Asparagus, peas and baby lettuce
Pumpkin and rice gratin
Creamy potato gratin
Carrots with crème fraîche and herbs
French beans with garlic
Cauliflower gratin
Ratatouille
Braised red cabbage
Spinach flan
Lesley Waters
New potato salad with gazpacho dressing
Broccoli trees with pan-fried pine nuts

PICTURES
Martin Brigdale
Pages 1, 8–9, 14, 18, 22, 30–31, 40, 44, 46, 57, 61
Peter Cassidy
Endpapers, pages 4–5, 13, 16–17, 29, 33, 50–51, 53
Nicky Dowey
Pages 5, 6–7
William Lingwood
Pages 2, 10, 20–21, 26–27, 36–37, 62
Ian Wallace
Pages 39, 43, 49
Philip Webb
Pages 24–25, 34–35, 54–55, 58